Bibliographic information published by the German National Library:

The German National Library lists this publication in the National Bibliography; detailed bibliographic data are available on the Internet at http://dnb.dnb.de .

Imprint:

Copyright © 2019 GRIN Verlag
Print and binding: Books on Demand GmbH, Norderstedt Germany
ISBN: 9783346039132

This book at GRIN:

https://www.grin.com/document/469095

Balamurugan Rengeswaran

A study on network intrusion detection using classifiers

GRIN Verlag

GRIN - Your knowledge has value

Since its foundation in 1998, GRIN has specialized in publishing academic texts by students, college teachers and other academics as e-book and printed book. The website www.grin.com is an ideal platform for presenting term papers, final papers, scientific essays, dissertations and specialist books.

A study on network intrusion detection using classifiers

Dr. R.Balamurugan

Associate Professor

School of Computer Science and Engineering
(SCOPE)

Vellore Institute of Technology, Vellore

Executive Summary

In these days of rising internet usage, almost everyone has access to the internet. It is available easily and readily. So along with increase in popularity and importance it also leads to an increase in risks and susceptibility to unwanted attacks. Networks and servers and more prone to malicious attacks than ever. Cyber security is vital in this age. Lots of organizations now interact and communicate with people via the internet. They store huge amounts of data in their computers or devices connected to the network. This data should only be accessed by authorized members of the organization. It is possible for hackers to gain unauthorized access to this data. A lot of sensitive information is present in the data which might lead to harm in the hands of hackers. It is important to protect the network from being attacked in such a way. Network security is an element of cyber security which aims to provide services so that the organizations are safe from such attacks. Intrusion detection systems are present in the network which work along with the firewalls to detect and prevent such attacks. For this project, we aim to identify the suitable machine learning technique to detect such attacks and which can be used in state of the art system.

CONTENTS	PAGE NO.
Executive Summary	ii
Table of contents	iii
List of figures	iv
List of Tables	vi
Abbreviations	vii
1. INTRODUCTION 1.1 Objective 1.2 Motivation 1.3 Background	1 1 1 1
2. WORK DESCRIPTION AND GOALS	3
3. TECHNICAL SPECIFICATION 3.1 Functional Requirements 3.2 Assumptions, Dependencies and Constraints 3.3 User Requirements and Product Specific System Requirements 3.4 Domain Requirements 3.5 Non-functional Requirements 3.6 Engineering Standard Requirements 3.7 System Requirements	5 5 5 5 5 5 6
4. DESIGN APPROACH AND DETAILS	8
5. SCHEDULE TASKS AND MILESTONES	17
6. DEMONSTRATION	17
7. RESULTS AND DISCUSSIONS	23
8. SUMMARY	28
9. REFERENCES	29

List of Figures

Figure No.	Title	Page No.
4.1	IDS Classification	8
4.2	Graph of Distribution of attacks	10
4.3	Histograms of Attributes	11
4.4	Skewness	12
4.5	Kurtosis	13
4.6	UML Diagram	14
4.7	DNN Architecture	14
4.8	LSTM Single Unit	15
4.9	Random Forest	16
4.10	Decision Tree	16
6.1	Load Dataset	17
6.2	Training Set Label Distribution	18
6.3	Testing Set Label Distribution	18
6.4	Categorical Features	19
6.5	Number of categories in each feature	19
6.6	Categorical Features converted into numerical	19
6.7	One Hot Encoder Implementation	19
6.8	Original Columns Dropped	20
6.9	Labels Converted into numbers	20
6.10	Save Preprocessed data	20
6.11	Load Feature Selection function	21
6.12	Seleckbest Scores	21
6.13	Import Libraries and processed data	22
6.14	Normalized Histogram	22
7.1	Naïve Bayes Performance Metrics	23
7.2	Naïve Bayes Confusion Matrix	23
7.3	Naïve Bayes Classification Report	23
7.4	Naïve Bayes ROC curve	24
7.5	Decision Tree Performance metrics	24
7.6	Decision Tree Confusion Matrix	24
7.7	Decision Tree Classification report	24

7.8	Decision Tree ROC curve	25
7.9	Random Forest Performance metrics	25
7.10	Random Forest Confusion Matrix	25
7.11	Random Forest Classification Report	25
7.12	Random Forest ROC curve	26
7.13	LSTM Performance metrics	26
7.14	LSTM Classification report	26
7.15	DNN Performance metrics	27
7.16	DNN Classification report	27

List of Tables

Table No.	Title	Page No.
3.1	Hardware Specifications	6
7.1	Comparison table of different classifiers	27

List of Abbreviations

IDS	Intrusion Detection System
DNN	Deep Neural Network
RNN	Recurrent Neural Networks
ML	Machine Learning
RAM	Random Access Memory
GPU	Graphics Processing Unit

1. INTRODUCTION

1.1. Objective

There are several intrusion detection systems in use today [7]. Researchers are trying to develop systems which use machine learning techniques to identify the signature of attackers [6]. This proposed system aims to find a suitable novel technique to be used as a backend to such a system.

1.2. Motivation

It is difficult or almost impossible to develop an intrusion detection system with 100 percent success rate. Most systems today have a lot of security flaws. Not all kinds of intrusions are known. Also, hackers are figuring out new ways into the networks using machine learning techniques [5]. Quick detection of these attacks will help to identify possible intruders. and limit damage effected. So, developing an efficient and accurate intrusion detection system will help to reduce network security threats.

1.3. Background

With the world trending towards being steadily reliant on computers and automation, it is a challenge to build networks and systems secure for everyday use. The number of security threats to organizations is increasing exponentially with the growth of online markets and services. They are numerous solutions to combat network security threats. Intrusion detection systems are placed alongside firewalls in networks to combat security threats. They scan the network for all the incoming and outgoing traffics and analyze the signature of the packets to detect whether they are malicious or normal. Machine learning is used to help the system learn the signature of known attacks and profile normal network packets [3]. Some of the best intrusion detection systems on the market are:

- Snort
- Bro
- OSSEC
- Suricata
- Sagan
- Security Onion
- Samhain

Most intrusion detection systems only detect attacks and make the intruders presence known to the systems. These are called passive intrusion detection systems. Other types of intrusion detection systems are active and reactive to the attack by discontinuing access or working with the network manager to reset the network settings.

The intrusion detection systems can be categorized in two ways. They can be categorized by how they are placed in the network. They are also categorized by whether they detect signatures or anomalies in the network.

By Position in the network:

Network Intrusion detection system: It is placed at different important points in the network so it can monitor the incoming and outgoing network packets for unwanted activity.

Host intrusion detection system: It is placed in all the systems which are directly connected to the network in question. It can detect unwanted network packets that are sent everywhere in the network including the local network. It is better than Network intrusion detection systems in this way. It also detects attacks originating from the system in which it is placed. Network Intrusion detection systems cannot monitor traffic in the local area network.

By type of detection:

Signature-based intrusion detection system: Signature based intrusion detection systems learn the signatures of different types of attacks which occur commonly and identify the right kind of attack on the system. The disadvantage of signature-based intrusion detection system is that they often fail to identify new types of attacks.

Anomaly-based intrusion detection system: Anomaly-based intrusion detection systems learn the characteristics of normal network packets and categorize anything not similar to normal as an anomaly. So Anomaly based intrusion detection systems are able to identify new types of attacks although they cannot identify the signature of specific attacks.

2. PROJECT DESCRIPTION AND GOALS

The project contains four modules: Data Preprocessing, Feature Selection, Training the models and Attack prediction and testing.

The dataset selected is NSL-KDD [2]. It is the refined version of the KDD Cup 99 dataset. The KDD Cup 99 dataset is one of the most widely used datasets for training Intrusion Detection Systems(IDS) and Intrusion Prevention Systems(IPS). There is a lack of labelled datasets for network security. This is because it is difficult to predict new types of attacks and know their signature. Some of the other popular datasets are DARPA, CAIDA, LBNL, CDX, Kyoto, UMASS, ISCX2012 and ADFA.

The KDD Cup 99 Dataset has a lot of redundant values and instances. The NSL-KDD is created after removing the redundant values. It has 41 attributes and is classified into 4 types of attacks along with the normal network packet values.

The next stage is Data Preprocessing. All the values in the dataset have to be in a numerical format for the classifiers to take in as input. Some of the features are categorical and have string values. This is then converted into numerical values using Label Encoder. A One-hot Encoder is then used to split the columns to each different category.

Next comes feature selection. Having a lot of unimportant features in the training set can hinder the accuracy of the predictive model. So the most important features contributing to the characteristics of the attack are chosen. There are several methods for feature selection.

1) Univariate Feature Selection
2) Recursive Feature Elimination
3) Principal Component Analysis

An optimal feature selection method has to be selected which is suitable for the dataset [9].

The next step is selecting and training various machine learning and deep learning models to analyze the best model for predicting malicious attacks [1]. One of the important requisites is to have model with a low false positive rate.

Three Machine learning models and two deep learning models are selected to train and test the dataset.

1) Random Forest
2) Decision Tree
3) Naïve Bayes

4) LSTM

5) Deep Neural Network

The dataset is split into 85% training and 15% testing and the above models are implemented. The performance metrics used will be

1) Accuracy

2) Precision

3) Recall

4) f1-score

The confusion matrix is also generated for all the models.

Deep learning models require a lot of computational power which is not present in most CPUs. So either GPUs or a cloud service should be used to train the model with the dataset. The latest datasets used are very large with a lot of redundant fields and it is required to preprocess the data and convert into format suitable for the model.

Goals

- Collecting a good dataset with huge amount of entries and appropriate risk factors.
- The acquired data cannot be used as it is. So, suitable data preparation techniques should be carried out in order to obtain accurate predictive models.
- The data is pruned for unwanted or unrelated attributes. It is then converted into numerical format so that the classifier can input the data.
- Feature extraction and feature selection should be performed as when we are dealing with large amounts of data, the most significant features become crucial.
- Implement several machine learning and deep learning techniques to identify the suitable algorithm for classification of the attacks.
- Achieve an accuracy above 75% in the testing phase.

3. REQUIREMENT ANALYSIS

3.1 Functional Requirements

3.1.1 Product Perspective

This product is for detecting network anomalies in traffic.

3.1.2 Product features

- High speed with such big data
- Compatible with most of the PCs
- The accuracy is also high

3.1.3 Assumption, Dependencies & Constraints

The names of the feature columns in the dataset will be different from the visualization layer. The model is dependent on all the feature columns given in the dataset.

3.1.4 Domain Requirements

Intrusion detection systems are placed alongside firewalls in networks. They are present in the host in Host Intrusion detection systems. In Network Intrusion detection systems they are distributed at critical points throughout the network.

3.2 Non Functional Requirements

Non-functional requirements are the requirements that do not directly show the specific functions of the system. They may specify system performance and maintainability and security.

System performance:

The user interface should be smooth and there should not be any crashes in the system.

Usability:

The system should be compatible with any PCs. It should work under any environment and also under any conditions.

Maintainability:

Preparing the software is not just the final. Maintenance is also an important thing. The maintenance cost should be less. Services should be available all the time without any interruptions.

Efficiency:

The output should be more accurate and should have a low false positive rate.

3.3 Engineering Standard Requirements (Explain the applicability for your work w.r.to the following operational requirement(s))

- **Economic**

Detecting and identifying hackers will prevent any losses to the companies hosting the networks.

- **Social**

The main aim of this project is to make it open source and it should be available to all the users.

- **Sustainability**

The system should work long enough with new developments doing to system time to time. It should adapt to the current systems by giving updates to the users which should increase the data clean and thus efficiency.

3.4 System Requirements

3.4.1 H/W Requirements(details about Application Specific Hardware)

Table 3.1 Hardware Specifications

Component	Spec
Core	4
RAM	16 GB
GPU	4 GB
Storage	500 GB
Operating system	Windows 10
Processor	I3 or higher

3.4.2 S/W Requirements(details about Application Specific Software)

1) Tensorflow-GPU Library
2) Keras API
3) Jupyter Notebook
4) NVIDIA CUDA Toolkit 10.1
5) NVIDIA cuDNN 7.0

4 DESIGN APPROACH AND DETAILS
4.1 Introduction

As discussed earlier the intrusion detection systems can be classified in two ways based on detection type and position.

In this project several machine learning and deep learning models are used to construct a system with good level of performance.

Anomaly-based intrusion detection system is selected for this project.

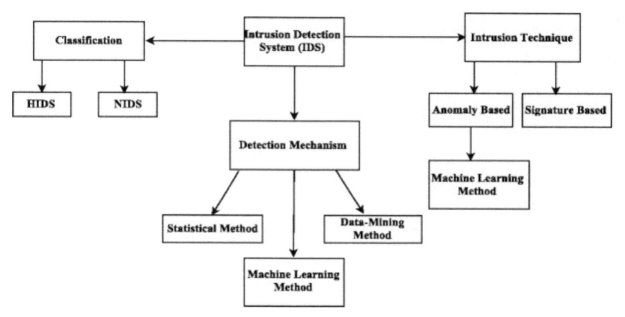

Figure 4.1 IDS Classification

The dataset used is the NSL-KDD. It is the refined version of KDD 99 dataset. Several thousand redundant samples are removed from the KDD 99 dataset to create the NSL-KDD dataset. The dataset is split into 85% for training set and 15% for testing set. The characteristics and details of the dataset will be discussed below along with the appropriate data preprocessing required to work with this dataset.

The dataset can be downloaded from the online repository in either ARFF or CSV format. We will use the csv format for reading in python environment.

Dataset Description and Details

The NSL-KDD dataset has 41 attributes or features. They are listed below.

1. duration
2. protocol type
3. service
4. flag
5. src bytes
6. dst bytes
7. land
8. wrong fragment
9. urgent
10. hot
11. num failed logins
12. logged in
13. num compromised
14. root shell
15. su attempted
16. num root,
17. num file creaticns,
18. num shells,
19. num access files,
20. num outbound cmds,
21. is host login,
22. is guest login,
23. count
24. srv count
25. serror_rate,
26. srv serror rate
27. rerror rate
28. srv rerror rate
29. same srv rate
30. diff srv rate

31. srv diff host rate

32. dst host count

33. dst host srv count

34. dst host same srv rate

35. dst host diff srv rate

36. dst host same src port rate

37. dst host srv diff host rate

38. dst host serror rate

39. dst host srv serror rate

40. dst host rerror rate

41. dst host srv rerror rate

42. label

The final attribute 'label' contains the classification of attacks. The distribution of each type of attack in the dataset in percentage is given below. Normal packets are the highest in number. The number of records in the NSL-KDD dataset are less compared to the KDD Cup 99. This makes it easier to run the model for all the samples rather than a selected set of samples. This makes the classifier unbiased as it is learning from all the available samples in the dataset.

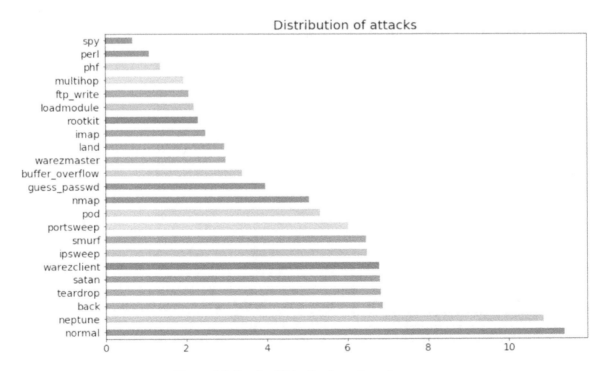

Figure 4.2 Graph of Distribution of attacks

Types of attacks recorded

1. Distributed Denial of Service (DDOS) – In a Distributed denial of service attack, the servers resources are depleted due to a large number of duplicate resource requests from the attack. This attack is carried out using multiple systems. The network server is bottlenecked due these requests and the services are stopped to legitimate users.

2. U2R – The attacker logs into the network using regular user credentials and tries to gain admin privilege by some sort of exploit. This is done by knowing the vulnerability in the system beforehand which the user has the knowledge of due to the attackers presence in the network.

3. R2L- The attacker tries to gain access to the network from a remote location. This is done by methods like password guessing, phishing, etc. The hacker tries to gain the user privilege.

4. Probe – The hacker sends a probe to scan the network for any weaknesses or points of entry.

The below graphs show the histograms of all the attributes in the datasets. It is noticeable that the values of the attributes are not normalized or scaled.

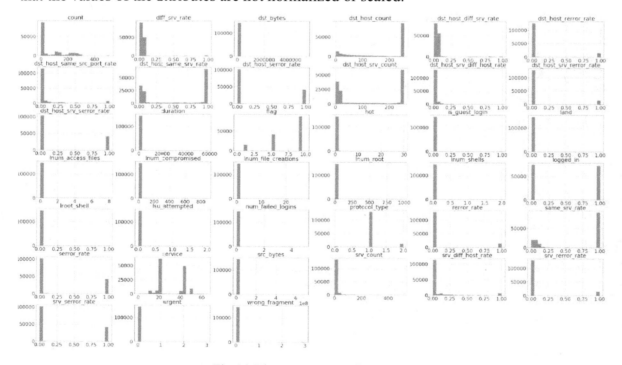

Fig 4.3 Histograms of Attributes

11

Skewness

```
duration                         15.617807
protocol_type                     1.604582
service                           0.097458
flag                             -0.987923
src_bytes                       379.577754
dst_bytes                        74.338368
land                             85.301818
wrong_fragment                   12.157263
urgent                          243.005916
hot                              18.076161
num_failed_logins                87.285356
logged_in                         0.034061
lnum_compromised                226.919396
lroot_shell                      51.420374
lsu_attempted                   125.381511
lnum_root                       226.412714
lnum_file_creations             104.414591
lnum_shells                      59.085797
lnum_access_files                33.260643
is_guest_login                   14.475562
count                             1.315556
srv_count                        10.868833
serror_rate                       0.921091
srv_serror_rate                   0.919544
rerror_rate                       2.517032
srv_rerror_rate                   2.526646
same_srv_rate                    -0.551576
diff_srv_rate                     6.412941
srv_diff_host_rate                2.987690
dst_host_count                   -0.794087
dst_host_srv_count                0.038799
dst_host_same_srv_rate           -0.154504
dst_host_diff_srv_rate            4.561781
dst_host_same_src_port_rate       3.030781
dst_host_srv_diff_host_rate       8.677578
dst_host_serror_rate              0.922716
dst_host_srv_serror_rate          0.923007
dst_host_rerror_rate              2.490536
dst_host_srv_rerror_rate          2.527145
```

Fig 4.4 Skewness

Kurtosis

duration	337.487126
protocol_type	6.201106
service	-1.488925
flag	-0.267043
src_bytes	144574.703142
dst_bytes	6002.858231
land	7274.500013
wrong_fragment	147.521554
urgent	64054.870180
hot	339.829748
num_failed_logins	10967.716784
logged_in	-1.998867
lnum_compromised	55522.171580
lroot_shell	2642.091159
lsu_attempted	16495.327964
lnum_root	55678.500406
lnum_file_creations	12843.768525
lnum_shells	3877.672299
lnum_access_files	2239.045398
is_guest_login	207.544743
count	1.099363
srv_count	147.594618
serror_rate	-1.146607
srv_serror_rate	-1.151628
rerror_rate	4.355662
srv_rerror_rate	4.410386
same_srv_rate	-1.659287
diff_srv_rate	44.648474
srv_diff_host_rate	7.913061
dst_host_count	-1.141875
dst_host_srv_count	-1.884692
dst_host_same_srv_rate	-1.889686
dst_host_diff_srv_rate	21.406849
dst_host_same_src_port_rate	8.001967
dst_host_srv_diff_host_rate	107.167834
dst_host_serror_rate	-1.143618
dst_host_srv_serror_rate	-1.146994
dst_host_rerror_rate	4.285796
dst_host_srv_rerror_rate	4.447453

Fig 4.5 Kurtosis

UML Diagram

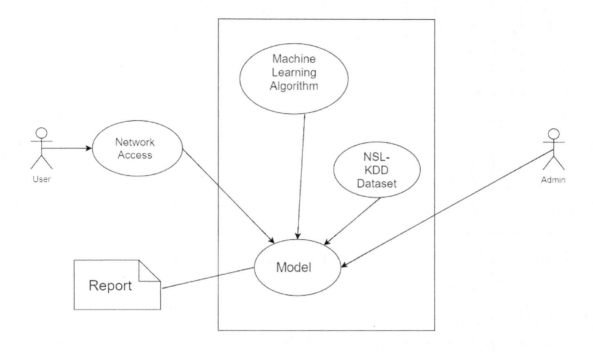

Fig 4.6 UML Diagram

Deep Neural Network

The deep neural network implemented has three hidden layers with 1024 neurons each. The input layer has 41 neurons. The output layer classifies the sample into either attack or not an attack.

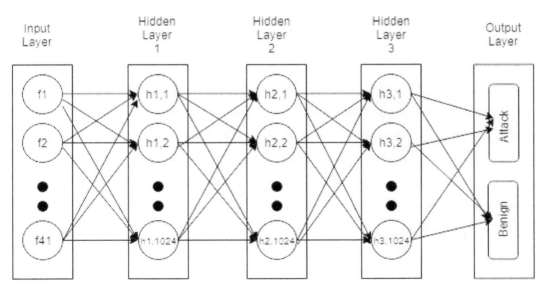

Fig 4.7 DNN Architecture

LSTM Model

LSTM or Long Short Term Memory is an RNN architecture. It is used in the field of deep learning. An LSTM unit consists of an input gate, output gate and a forget gate. LSTM networks are useful for classification problems.

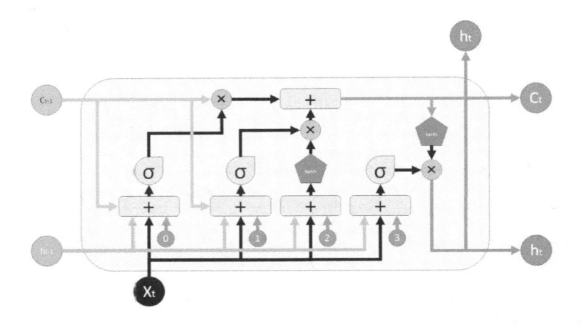

Fig 4.8 LSTM single unit

Random Forest Classifier

Random forest classifier or Random decision forest is a popular classification algorithm used in machine learning. It is an ensemble algorithm. It creates a set of decision trees to calculate information gain of all the features extracted.

It uses the weights from all the decision trees to classify a particular sample into a result. A single decision tree may be impacted by outliers or noise. But by using an ensemble of decision trees a random forest classifier can significantly improve performance.

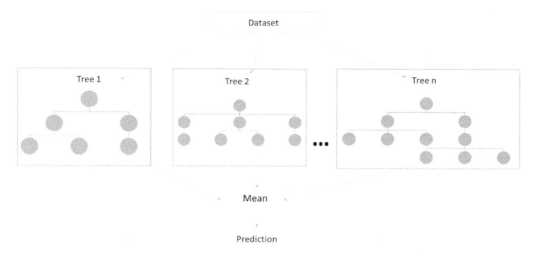

Fig 4.9 Random Forest

Decision Tree Classifier

Decision Tree Classifier builds a systematic approach for classification. It uses information gain and entropy to build a predictive model. It is built recursively by selecting subsets of features and finding the relationship between the feature and the class.

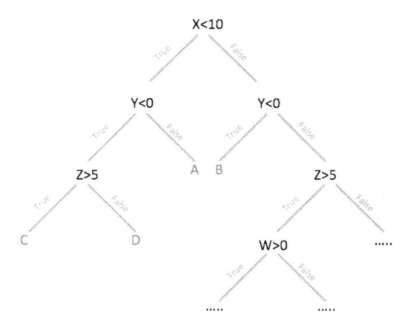

Fig 4.10 Decision Tree

6. PROJECT DEMONSTRATION

Data pre-processing

For data pre-processing, we have to follow some steps. They are:

1. Import all the required libraries

2. Import the data

3. Check for missing values and outliers

4. Process the data with suitable techniques

5. Data splitting

For building a good predictive model, data cleaning must be done. Data might not be very clean containing some outliers and missing values. So, we have to process the data for using to develop the model. In machine learning the data pre-processing is crucial part which effects the accuracy of the output. We have to import all the required ML libraries. Then read the data by giving the location the data. Check for the missing values and outliers if present in the data. So, the data pre-processing should be done using suitable techniques.

The libraries mainly used for data preprocessing are scikit-learn, pandas, numpy and matplotlib. scikit-learn contains several functions for processing data. pandas is used to load the data into dataframes and numpy is used to process the data in numpy arrays. matplotlib is used for data visualization.

In the NSL-KDD dataset the dataset is first loaded from local memory.

```
In [16]: import pandas as pd
         import numpy as np
         import matplotlib
         import matplotlib.pyplot as plt

In [17]: col_names = ["duration","protocol_type","service","flag","src_bytes",
             "dst_bytes","land","wrong_fragment","urgent","hot","num_failed_logins",
             "logged_in","num_compromised","root_shell","su_attempted","num_root",
             "num_file_creations","num_shells","num_access_files","num_outbound_cmds",
             "is_host_login","is_guest_login","count","srv_count","serror_rate",
             "srv_serror_rate","rerror_rate","srv_rerror_rate","same_srv_rate",
             "diff_srv_rate","srv_diff_host_rate","dst_host_count","dst_host_srv_count",
             "dst_host_same_srv_rate","dst_host_diff_srv_rate","dst_host_same_src_port_rate",
             "dst_host_srv_diff_host_rate","dst_host_serror_rate","dst_host_srv_serror_rate",
             "dst_host_rerror_rate","dst_host_srv_rerror_rate","label"]

         df = pd.read_csv("KDDTrain+_2.csv", header=None, names = col_names)
         df_test = pd.read_csv("KDDTest+_2.csv", header=None, names = col_names)

         print('Dimensions of the Training set:',df.shape)
         print('Dimensions of the Test set:',df_test.shape)

         Dimensions of the Training set: (125973, 42)
         Dimensions of the Test set: (22544, 42)
```

Fig 6.1 Load dataset

The distribution of the attacks can then be viewed.

```
Label distribution Training set:
normal            67343
neptune           41214
satan              3633
ipsweep            3599
portsweep          2931
smurf              2646
nmap               1493
back                956
teardrop            892
warezclient         890
pod                 201
guess_passwd         53
buffer_overflow      30
warezmaster          20
land                 18
imap                 11
rootkit              10
loadmodule            9
ftp_write             8
multihop              7
phf                   4
perl                  3
spy                   2
```

Fig 6.2 Training set Label Distribution

```
Label distribution Test set:
normal             9711
neptune            4657
guess_passwd       1231
mscan               996
warezmaster         944
apache2             737
satan               735
processtable        685
smurf               665
back                359
snmpguess           331
saint               319
mailbomb            293
snmpgetattack       178
portsweep           157
ipsweep             141
httptunnel          133
nmap                 73
pod                  41
buffer_overflow      20
multihop             18
named                17
ps                   15
sendmail             14
xterm                13
rootkit              13
teardrop             12
xlock                 9
land                  7
xsnoop                4
ftp_write             3
udpstorm              2
worm                  2
phf                   2
perl                  2
loadmodule            2
sqlattack             2
imap                  1
```

Fig 6.3 Testing set Label Distribution

The dataset has several categorical features in non-numerical values. The columns protocol_type, service and flag are non-numerical.

	protocol_type	service	flag
0	tcp	ftp_data	SF
1	udp	other	SF
2	tcp	private	S0
3	tcp	http	SF
4	tcp	http	SF

Fig 6.4 Categorical Features

The following figure shows the number of categories.

```
Training set:
Feature 'protocol_type' has 3 categories
Feature 'service' has 70 categories
Feature 'flag' has 11 categories
Feature 'label' has 23 categories

Test set:
Feature 'protocol_type' has 3 categories
Feature 'service' has 64 categories
Feature 'flag' has 11 categories
Feature 'label' has 38 categories
```

Fig 6.5 Number of categories in each categorical feature

These categories are converted into numerical data using LabelEncoder.

```
  protocol_type  service  flag
0             1       20     9
1             2       44     9
2             1       49     5
3             1       24     9
4             1       24     9
```

Fig 6.6 Categorical Features converted to numerical

These categorical features are then converted to binary vectors in different columns using One hot Encoder.

```
enc = OneHotEncoder()
df_categorical_values_encenc = enc.fit_transform(df_categorical_values_enc)
df_cat_data = pd.DataFrame(df_categorical_values_encenc.toarray(),columns=dumcols)
# test set
testdf_categorical_values_encenc = enc.fit_transform(testdf_categorical_values_enc)
testdf_cat_data = pd.DataFrame(testdf_categorical_values_encenc.toarray(),columns=testdumcols)

df_cat_data.head()
```

Fig 6.7 One hot Encoder implementation

The new columns are given names and the original columns are dropped

```
newdf=df.join(df_cat_data)
newdf.drop('flag', axis=1, inplace=True)
newdf.drop('protocol_type', axis=1, inplace=True)
newdf.drop('service', axis=1, inplace=True)
# test data
newdf_test=df_test.join(testdf_cat_data)
newdf_test.drop('flag', axis=1, inplace=True)
newdf_test.drop('protocol_type', axis=1, inplace=True)
newdf_test.drop('service', axis=1, inplace=True)
print(newdf.shape)
print(newdf_test.shape)

(125973, 123)
(22544, 123)
```

Fig 6.8 Original Columns dropped

The labels are then converted into 5 classes in numerical format.

```
# take label column
labeldf=newdf['label']
labeldf_test=newdf_test['label']
# change the label column
newlabeldf=labeldf.replace({ 'normal' : 0, 'neptune' : 1 ,'back': 1, 'land': 1, 'pod': 1, 'smurf': 1, 'teardrop': 1,'mailbomb':
                            'ipsweep' : 2,'nmap' : 2,'portsweep' : 2,'satan' : 2,'mscan' : 2,'saint' : 2
                            ,'ftp_write': 3,'guess_passwd': 3,'imap': 3,'multihop': 3,'phf': 3,'spy': 3,'warezclient': 3,'warezma
                            'buffer_overflow': 4,'loadmodule': 4,'perl': 4,'rootkit': 4,'ps': 4,'sqlattack': 4,'xterm': 4})
newlabeldf_test=labeldf_test.replace({ 'normal' : 0, 'neptune' : 1 ,'back': 1, 'land': 1, 'pod': 1, 'smurf': 1, 'teardrop': 1,'m
                            'ipsweep' : 2,'nmap' : 2,'portsweep' : 2,'satan' : 2,'mscan' : 2,'saint' : 2
                            ,'ftp_write': 3,'guess_passwd': 3,'imap': 3,'multihop': 3,'phf': 3,'spy': 3,'warezclient': 3,'warezma
                            'buffer_overflow': 4,'loadmodule': 4,'perl': 4,'rootkit': 4,'ps': 4,'sqlattack': 4,'xterm': 4})
# put the new label column back
newdf['label'] = newlabeldf
newdf_test['label'] = newlabeldf_test
print(newdf['label'].head(100))
```

Fig 6.9 Labels converted to numbers

The dataset is then stored in csv format in separate files for classes and input attributes.

```
newdf=newdf.drop('label',1)
newdf_test=newdf_test.drop('label',1)


xtrain=newdf.values
xtest=newdf_test.values


np.savetxt("ktrain.csv", xtrain, delimiter=",",fmt='%01d')
np.savetxt("ktest.csv", xtest, delimiter=",",fmt='%01d')
np.savetxt("trainlabel.csv",trainlabel,delimiter=",",fmt='%01d')
np.savetxt("testlabel.csv",testlabel,delimiter=",",fmt='%01d')
```

Fig 6.10 Save Preprocessed Data

Feature Selection

Univariate Feature selection is used to select 19 best features to train the machine learning models [8].

```
from sklearn.feature_selection import SelectKBest
from sklearn.feature_selection import f_regression

selectkbest = SelectKBest(score_func=f_regression, k=19)

sfit = selectkbest.fit(xtrain,trainlabel)
```

Fig 6.11 Load Feature Selection Function

The scores of the function are then viewed to select best 19.

	Specs	Score
29	dst_host_srv_count	80429.505583
8	logged_in	62555.256279
120	flag_SF	54247.441673
30	dst_host_same_srv_rate	48141.434312
65	service_http	44636.075036
25	same_srv_rate	44487.974220
90	service_private	23832.482390
31	dst_host_diff_srv_rate	22779.211010
19	count	22373.586292
35	dst_host_srv_serror_rate	21894.054387
34	dst_host_serror_rate	21538.475438
21	serror_rate	21476.242007
22	srv_serror_rate	21086.626567
116	flag_S0	20428.440217
55	service_eco_i	16286.180493
32	dst_host_same_src_port_rate	14280.701881
37	dst_host_srv_rerror_rate	13414.601691
24	srv_rerror_rate	13384.129264
23	rerror_rate	13265.969486

Fig 6.12 selectkbest scores

Training the models

The first step of training the models is to import the required libraries and processed dataset.

```python
import numpy as np
import pandas as pd
from sklearn.kernel_approximation import RBFSampler
from sklearn.linear_model import SGDClassifier
from sklearn.model_selection import train_test_split
from sklearn import svm
from sklearn.metrics import classification_report
from sklearn import metrics
from sklearn.linear_model import LogisticRegression
from sklearn.naive_bayes import GaussianNB
from sklearn.neighbors import KNeighborsClassifier
from sklearn.tree import DecisionTreeClassifier
from sklearn.metrics import (precision_score, recall_score,f1_score, accuracy_score,mean_squared_error,mean_absolute_error)
from sklearn.ensemble import AdaBoostClassifier
from sklearn.ensemble import RandomForestClassifier
from sklearn.preprocessing import Normalizer
from sklearn.model_selection import GridSearchCV
from sklearn.svm import SVC
from sklearn.metrics import confusion_matrix
from sklearn.metrics import (precision_score, recall_score,f1_score, accuracy_score,mean_squared_error,mean_absolute_error,


traindata = pd.read_csv('ktrain1.csv', header=None)
testdata = pd.read_csv('ktest1.csv', header=None)
```

Fig 6.13 Import libraries and processed data

The data is then normalized.

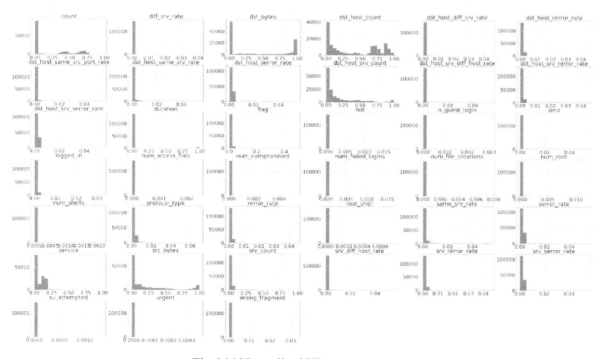

Fig 6.14 Normalized Histogram

The models are then fitted on the training set and target values.
The testing phase is done after the training and is done on the test set.

7. RESULTS AND DISCUSSION

Naïve Bayes

```
accuracy
0.738
precision
0.876
racall
0.628
f1score
0.732
```

Fig 7.1 Naïve Bayes Performance metrics

Predicted attacks	0	1
Actual attacks		
0	8573	1138
1	4772	8061

Fig 7.2 Naïve Bayes Confusion Matrix

	precision	recall	f1-score	support
0	0.64	0.88	0.74	9711
1	0.88	0.63	0.73	12833
micro avg	0.74	0.74	0.74	22544
macro avg	0.76	0.76	0.74	22544
weighted avg	0.78	0.74	0.74	22544

Fig 7.3 Naïve Bayes Classification Report

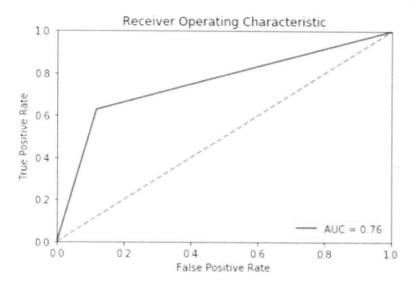

Fig 7.4 Naïve Bayes ROC curve

Decision Tree

```
accuracy
0.769
precision
0.957
racall
0.622
f1score
0.754
```

Fig 7.5 Decision Tree Performance Metrics

Predicted attacks	0	1
Actual attacks		
0	9353	358
1	4846	7987

Fig 7.6 Decision Tree Confusion Matrix

```
              precision    recall   f1-score    support

           0       0.66      0.96       0.78       9711
           1       0.96      0.62       0.75      12833

   micro avg       0.77      0.77       0.77      22544
   macro avg       0.81      0.79       0.77      22544
weighted avg       0.83      0.77       0.77      22544
```

Fig 7.7 Decision Tree Classification Report

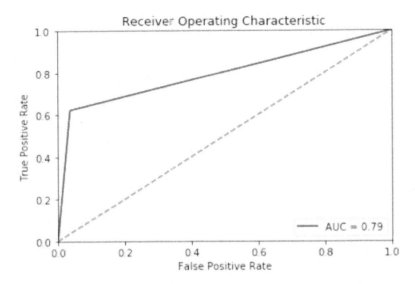

Fig 7.8 Decision Tree ROC Curve

Random Forest

```
accuracy
0.758
precision
0.966
racall
0.597
f1score
0.738
```

Fig 7.9 Random Forest Performance Metrics

Predicted attacks	0	1
Actual attacks		
0	9443	268
1	5177	7656

Fig 7.10 Random Forest Confusion Matrix

```
              precision   recall   f1-score   support

           0      0.65      0.97       0.78       9711
           1      0.97      0.60       0.74      12833

   micro avg      0.76      0.76       0.76      22544
   macro avg      0.81      0.78       0.76      22544
weighted avg      0.83      0.76       0.75      22544
```

Fig 7.11 Random Forest Classification Report

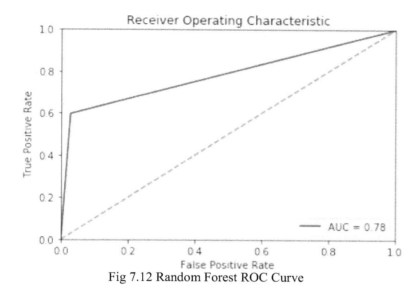

Fig 7.12 Random Forest ROC Curve

LSTM

```
accuracy
0.768
recall
0.613
precision
0.968
f1score
0.750
```

Fig 7.13 LSTM Performance Metrics

	precision	recall	f1-score	support
0	0.66	0.97	0.78	9711
1	0.97	0.61	0.75	12833
micro avg	0.77	0.77	0.77	22544
macro avg	0.81	0.79	0.77	22544
weighted avg	0.83	0.77	0.76	22544

Fig 7.14 LSTM Classification Report

DNN

```
accuracy
0.776
recall
0.627
precision
0.970
f1score
0.761
```

Fig 7.15 DNN Performance Metrics

```
              precision    recall  f1-score   support

           0       0.66      0.97      0.79      9711
           1       0.97      0.63      0.76     12833

   micro avg       0.78      0.78      0.78     22544
   macro avg       0.82      0.80      0.78     22544
weighted avg       0.84      0.78      0.77     22544
```

Fig 7.16 DNN Classification Report

Table 7.1 Comparison table of Different Classifiers

Algorithm	Accuracy	Precision	Recall	f1-score
Naïve Bayes	0.738	0.876	0.628	0.732
Decision Tree	0.769	0.957	0.622	0.754
Random Forest	0.760	0.966	0.599	0.740
DNN 3 layer	0.776	0.970	0.627	0.761
LSTM	0..768	0.968	0.613	0.750

The above table shows the comparison of different classifiers based on the performance metrics accuracy, precision, recall and f1-score. DNN-3 Layer has the highest accuracy of all the classifiers. Naïve Bayes has the lowest accuracy as well as precision values.

5 SUMMARY

The dataset NSL-KDD was selected due to its ease of use and adaptability. It is also rigorous and easily available and highly researched. Random Forest, Naïve Bayes, Decision Tree were the machine learning models selected for the intrusion detection system. These models are very popular and have a high level of performance in many areas of computer science. Hence, they were selected. Two deep learning models were selected: Deep neural network model and LSTM Model. The dataset was first preprocessed and cleaned. Feature selection was done using univariate feature selection. After selection of the features all the models are trained using this NSL-KDD preprocessed dataset. The training testing split was 85-15. After evaluating performance using metrics like accuracy, precision, recall, f1-score and the ROC curve. DNN is found to have higher accuracy than the other models. It is hoped that more research will help fine tune this model and improve the accuracy even more for use in open source systems as a backend.

8. REFERENCES

[1] Chuanlong Yin, Jinlong Fei, Yuefei Zhu and Xinzheng He. A Deep Learning Approach for Intrusion detection using Recurrent Neural Networks. IEEE Access Volume 5. 5th October 2017

[2] Mahbod Tavallaee, Ebrahim Bagheri, Wei Lu, Ali A. Ghorbani. A detailed analysis of the KDD CUP 99 data set. CISDA'09.

[3] Phurivit Sangkatsanee, Chalermpol Charnsripinyo and Naruemon Wattanapongsakorn. Practice real-time intrusion detection using machine learning approaches. Computer Communications 34 2011

[4] Gisung Kim, Sehun Kim and Seungmin Lee. An novel hybrid intrusion detection method integrating anomaly detection with misuse detection. Expert systems with Applications 41 2014

[5] Muna AL-Hawawreh, Elena Sitnikova and Nour Moustafa. Identification of malicious activities in industrial internet of things based on deep learning models. Journal of Information Security and Applications 41(2018)

[6] Manjula C. Belavagi and Balachandra Muniyal. Performance Evaluation of Supervised Machine Learning Algorithms for Intrusion Detection. Procedia Computer Science 89 (2016).

[7] Hung-Jen Liao, Chun-Hung Richard Lin, Kuang-Yuan Tung, Ying-Chih Lin. Intrusion Detection System: A Comprehensive Review. Journal of Network and Computer Applications Vol 36, January 2013

[8] Fabian Pedregosa, Matthieu Brucher Gaël Varoquaux, Vincent Michel, Alexandre Passos Bertrand Thirion, Mathieu Blondel, Peter Prettenhofer, Ron Weiss, Vincent Dubourg, Jake Vanderplas, Alexandre Gramfort, David Cournapeau, Matthieu Perrot, Édouard Duchesnay, Olivier Grisel. Scikit-learn: Machine Learning in Python. JMLR 2011

[9] M.Dash, H.Liu. Feature Selection for Classification. Intelligent Data Analysis. Volume 1, 1997.